Exploring the Genius of da Vinci through Scavenger Hunts

Catherine McGrew Jaime

Other Da Vinci Books by Catherine Jaime

- *Da Vinci: His Life and His Legacy*
- *Doing Da Vinci For Kids*
- *In Art: Leonardo*
- *Exploring Da Vinci's Last Supper*
- *Leonardo da Vinci Topical Study*
- *The Life & Travels of Da Vinci Trilogy* (historical fiction)
- *Leonardo the Florentine* (historical fiction)
- *Leonardo: Masterpieces in Milan* (historical fiction)
- *Leonardo: To Mantua and Beyond* (historical fiction)

Creative Learning Connection

8006 Old Madison Pike, Ste 11-A

Madison, AL 35758

www.CreativeLearningConnection.com

All rights reserved. Permission is granted for the scavenger hunts to be reproduced for use by one family or class.

Copyright 2014 Catherine M. Jaime

www.CatherineJaime.com

Coloring pictures and pictures of paintings are used by permission of Dover Publications.

Table of Contents

Introduction 5

Leonardo Da Vinci Scavenger Hunt: Enter the World of Leonardo da Vinci! 7

Renaissance Paintings Scavenger Hunt 11

A Closer Look at Leonardo's Paintings 15

Approximate Dates for Leonardo's Paintings/Drawings 17

Mona Lisa 19

Scavenger Hunt 19

Leonardo da Vinci and Human Anatomy 21

Leonardo's Last Supper Q and A 23

Leonardo da Vinci and Animals 25

Leonardo and His Horse Sculpture Scavenger Hunt 27

Hydraulic and Aquatic Studies 31

A Sample of Leonardo Quotes 33

My Notes and Sketches 35

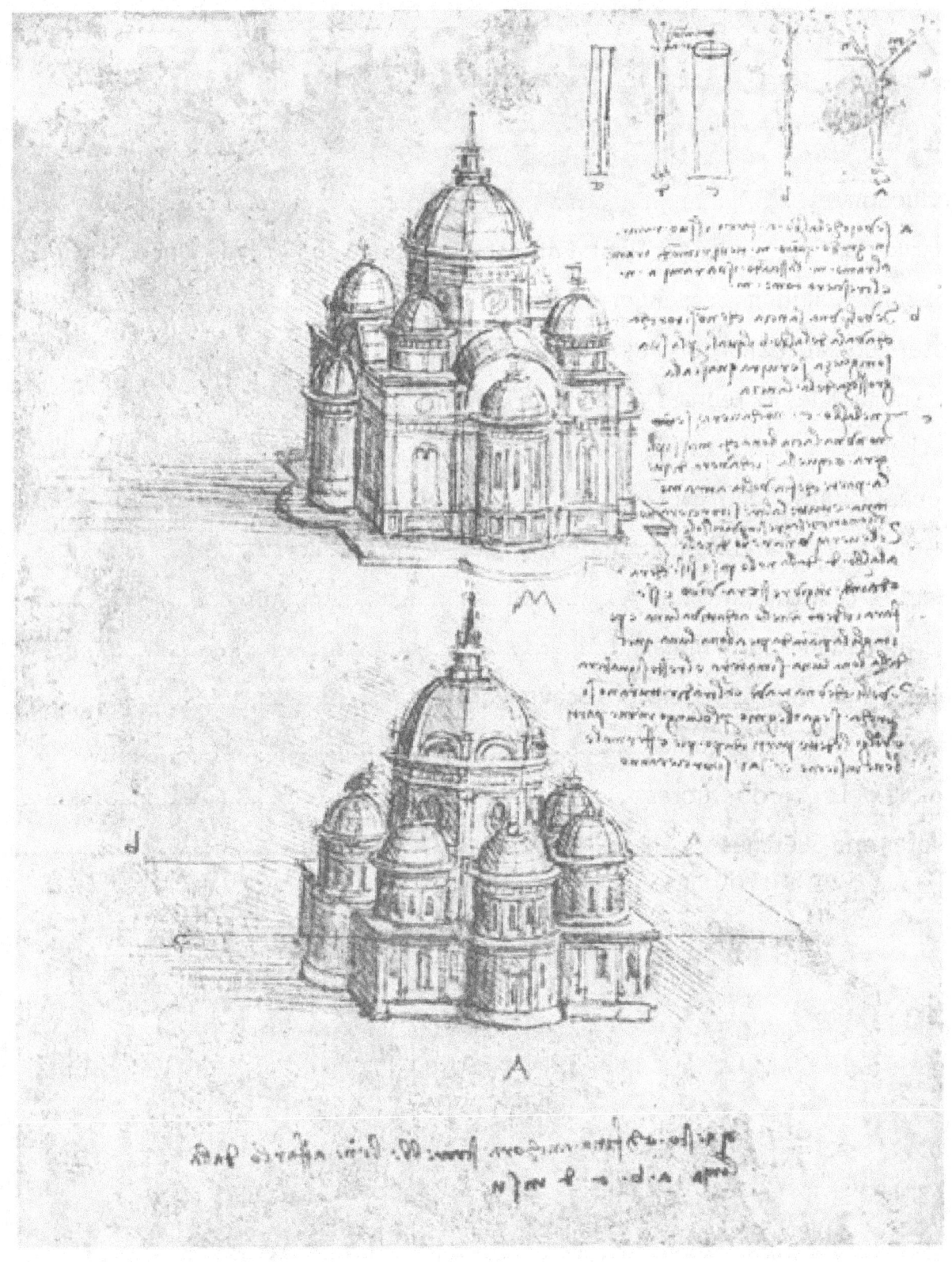

Leonardo studied Architecture.

Introduction

Leonardo was a great painter, but he was so much more. As you'll soon see, his interests clearly covered many other areas. Through these different scavenger hunts students can get a better idea of the types of topics Leonardo studied. The hunts were originally written to help students enjoy a specific exhibit on the genius of da Vinci, but they have been redone for use by students who cannot attend the physical exhibit. You can find most of the answers on our website: http://www.creativelearningconnection.com/daVinci.html.

The first hunt is a general hunt, to give students an idea of what Leonardo accomplished in his lifetime! Each of the other hunts focus on a specific areas – they do not need to be done in any particular order.

Happy Hunting!

Cathy

My Notes and Sketches

Leonardo Da Vinci Scavenger Hunt: Enter the World of Leonardo da Vinci!

See if you can find (and then draw) an example from each category below:

Leonardo, the Artist	Leonardo, a Civil Engineer
Leonardo, Military Advisor	**Leonardo, the Scientist**

Leonardo's work as a Sculptor:
Do you know what type of large sculpture Leonardo attempted in Milan?   Was it to be life size?

Check the **Timeline of Leonardo's Life and Time:**
　　　　Approximately how many years ago did he live?
Where was Leonardo born?   Where was he living at the end of his life?

Leonardo and Flight
Leonardo once said of flight: *"There shall be wings! If the accomplishment be not for me, 'tis for some other."* What do you think he meant by that?

Apparently Leonardo first considered the options of flight as a valuable resource for military operations (particularly to keep an eye on what one's enemy was up to), so you will need to go to the Military Advisor page to see some of his flight designs. Leonardo studied bats and birds for his ideas. He once wrote of one of his designs: *"...but be sure that the force is rapid and if the above effect is not obtained, waste no more time on it."*

The Wright Brothers finally flew in 1903.
Approximately how much earlier had Leoanrdo dreamed of humans flying?

Anatomical Studies
Did you know that no one had ever drawn the human body like this?
Which sketch do you like the most?

Leonardo and Bridges:
If you have Lincoln Logs, you may be able to put together Leonardo's "emergency bridge" yourself.
Closely examine the different **Bridges**. Which you do you like best? Sketch it:

Leonardo once wrote: "I have been impressed with the urgency of doing. Knowing is not enough; we must apply. Being willing is not enough; we must do." (Do you think he followed through on that philosophy?)

We can also look at sketches of many of Leonardo's **Military Inventions**. For someone who hated war, he had many ideas for war machines. Draw one below. (Do you think it would have worked?)

Leonardo drew the **map of Imola** while he was working as a military advisor for the ruthless Cesare Brogia. Can you find the castle, the city walls, and the river in Leonardo's "bird's eye" view of Imola?

After the plague in Milan, Leonardo planned an **Ideal City**. Find the sketches of it. What was an important aspect of his planned city?

Look at **Leonardo's Paintings and Drawings**. These are most of the ones that are generally attributed in part or in whole to Leonardo. Which you do you like best?

Compare the portraits Leonardo painted of women. Name at least one similarity and difference between them.

The Last Supper:
What can you see on the table in front of the disciples?

What colors are in the robe Jesus is wearing?

How long did it take Leonardo to paint this?

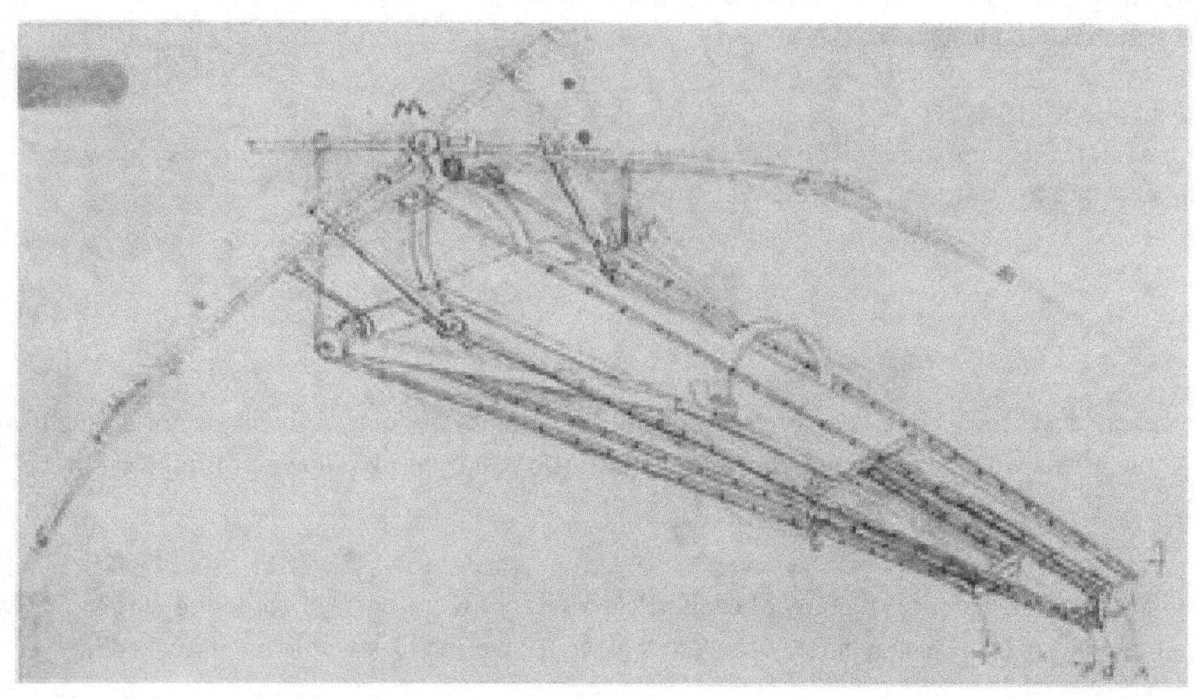

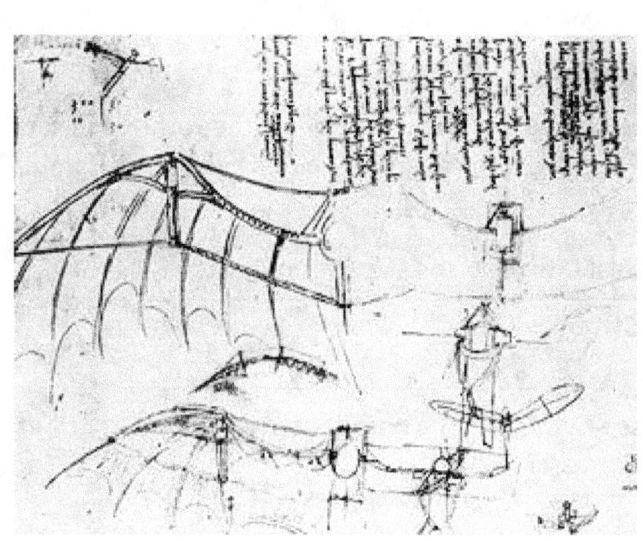
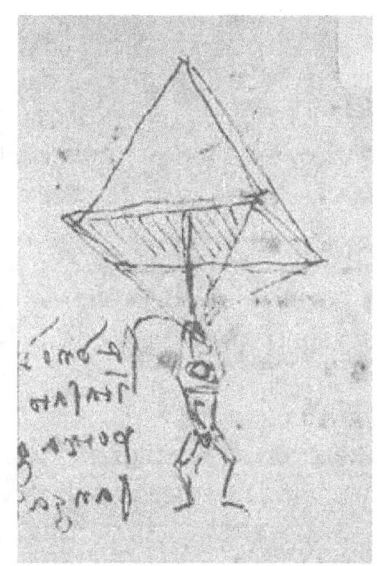

Leonard's Flight Studies

Leonardo once wrote: *"There shall be wings! If the accomplishment be not for me, 'tis for some other."*

Renaissance Paintings Scavenger Hunt

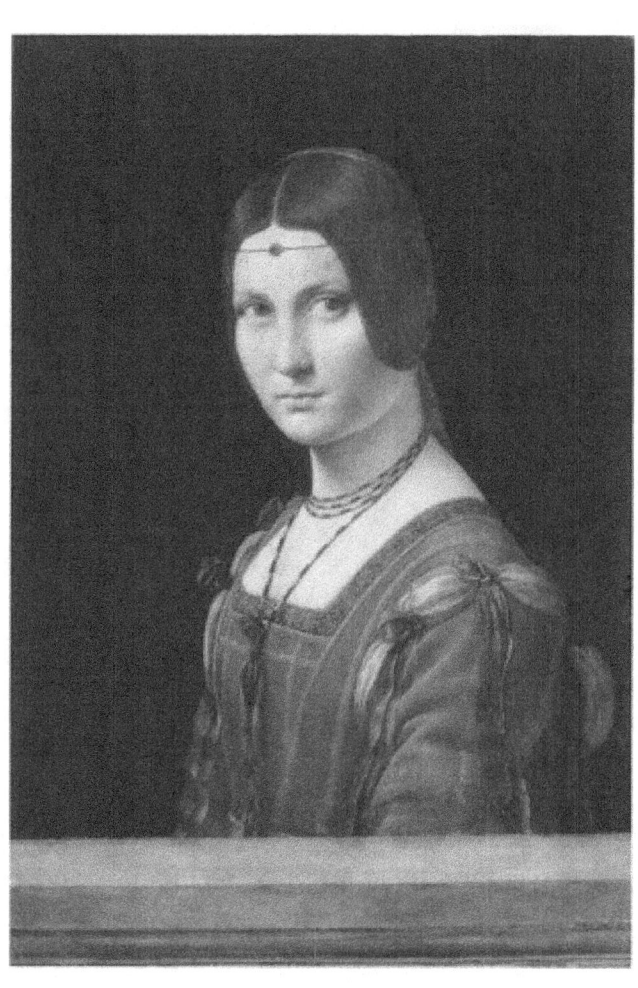

Start by examining the pictures on the Paintings portion of the website.

How many of them are sketches? ☐   How many of them are paintings? ☐

Now, begin with the sketches. One of the sketches is called a "cartoon" – it was a plan for an altarpiece painting. Can you tell which one it was? Name or sketch it here:

One of the sketches is a self-portrait (or as I heard it called the other day, a "selfie").
Try your hand at sketching Leonardo's self-portrait: Try making your own self-portrait:

Going back to the paintings themselves:
During the Renaissance, paintings were generally divided into two groups, religious or portraits.

How many religious paintings do you see among Leonardo's? ☐
How many portraits? ☐

On close examination, two of the paintings seem incomplete. Pick one and explain or sketch why:

Looking at the portraits, do you notice that all of the women except one are almost facing you?
It was unusual in Leonardo's day to paint women that way – it was typical to paint them in profile.
Which one of these is in profile? [ ]

How many of the women have some sort of a band around their head? [ ]

How many women are clearly wearing jewelry? [ ]   In how many paintings can you see plants? [ ]

What do you see in the background of most of Leonardo's paintings?
[ ]

Religious paintings of the day generally included halos – did all of Leonardo's? [ ]

You can only see one of these actual paintings without leaving the U.S.
Do you know which one and where is it?
[ ] [ ]

If you ever get to see that painting be sure to go around it and see the back:

Do you think the women in the portraits are rich or poor? Why?
[ ] [ ]

Which of Leonardo's paintings are most famous?
[ ] [ ]

Which painting do you like the best and why?
[ ]

My Notes and Sketches

A Closer Look at Leonardo's Paintings

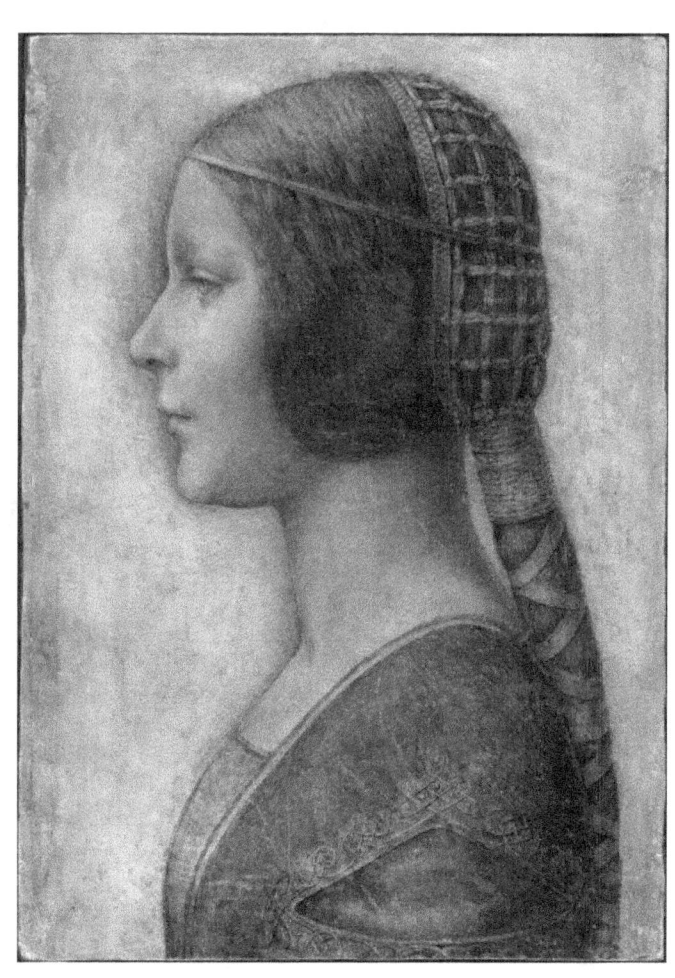

These copies of Leonardo's paintings are not displayed exactly in chronological order here, but they're close. Look closely at the five paintings Leonardo did during **his early years in Florence** (starting with the first one, the Annunciation, and ending with the fifth one, St. Jerome). Look closely at those five paintings. What do you notice about most about these and their backgrounds?

What other similarities and differences do you notice in this group?

The second group of six paintings are all believed to be from **the first time Leonardo lived in Milan**. (This is the same timeframe that he worked on his equestrian sculpture.) These paintings, starting with the sixth one, La Belle Frerronniere and going through the first Virgin of the Rocks have similarities with each other and differences from the first group. List one or more of each:

Look closely at both versions of the Virgin of the Rocks.
What are some differences between them?

Skipping the second Virgin of the Rocks (which he probably returned to Milan even later to do), the next three pictures were probably done when Leonardo returned to Florence after having been gone for eighteen years. What are some similarities and differences in these three?

Going back to his earliest Madonnas from his first time in Florence, compare those with his latter pictures of the Holy Family, when he's back in Florence. What similarities/differences do you notice?

Approximate Dates for Leonardo's Paintings/Drawings

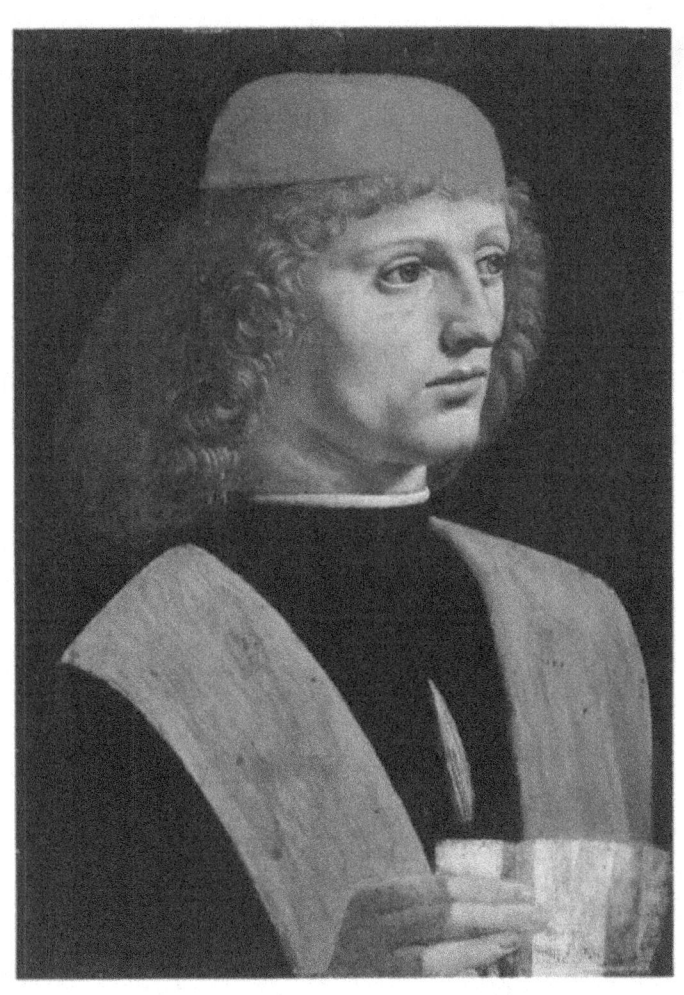

Approximate Dates for Leonardo's Paintings/Drawings*

1st Florence	1472 – 1475	The Annunciation (first complete work)
	1474 – 1478	Ginevra de'Benci
	1478 – 1480	Madonna of the Carnation
	1478 - 1481	Benois Madonna
	1480 - 1482	St. Jerome
1st Milan	1483 - 1485	Virgin of the Rocks (Louvre version)
	1485	Vitruvian Man
	1490	La Belle Ferroniere
	1490	Portrait of a Musician
	1490 – 1491	Lady with an Ermine
	1495 – 1496	La Bella Principessa
	1495 – 1498	The Last Supper
Florence	1500	Virgin and Child with St. Anne Cartoon
(w/Borgia)	1502	Map of Imola
Back to Florence	1503 – 1507	Mona Lisa
	1504 – 1505	Battle of Anghiara
Milan	~1508?	2nd Virgin of the Rocks (London version)
	1510	Virgin and Child with St. Anne
	1510	Self-portrait
Rome	1513 – 1516	St. John the Baptist (his last painting)

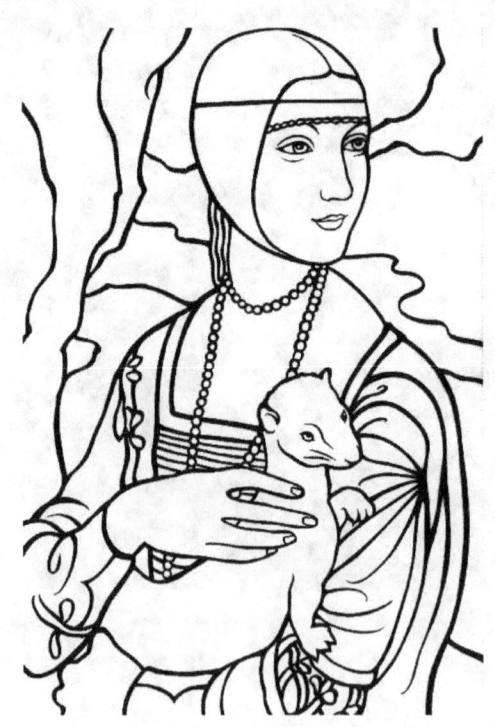

*This is not a complete list of Leonardo's paintings, though it is probably close.

Mona Lisa Scavenger Hunt

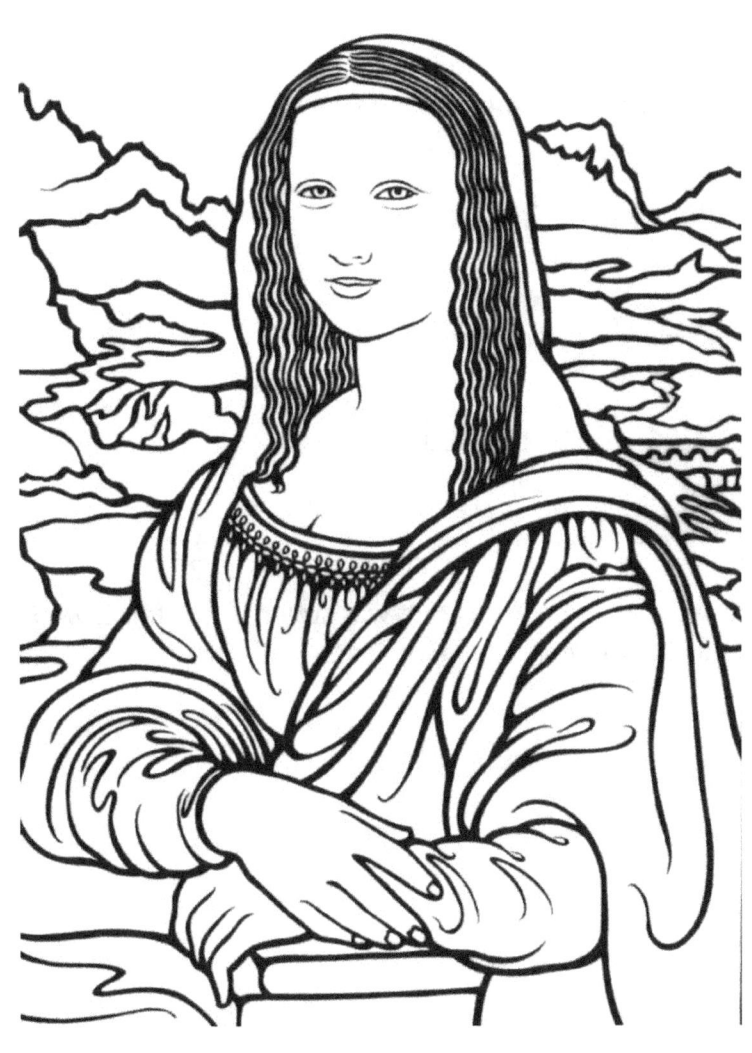

Leonardo painted the Mona Lisa on poplar wood, with oil paints (his usual type of paints).

List or draw what can you see in the background behind Mona Lisa?:

Can you see part of a piece of furniture in the painting?
What is it?

What is she wearing on her head?

Look closely at the far sides of the painting, do you see the portion of two columns there? (Because of those, it was once thought that the painting had been cut, but now the belief is that the painting is the original size.)

Do you see the bridge in the background? It's an old Roman bridge Leonardo most likely saw and sketched while he was working for Cesare Borgia.

When and where did Leonardo start painting the Mona Lisa?

Where do you have to go now to see it?

Did you know the Mona Lisa was stolen in 1911? It was stolen by an Italian who thought it should be returned to Italy. It was missing for more than two years.

Leonardo da Vinci and Human Anatomy

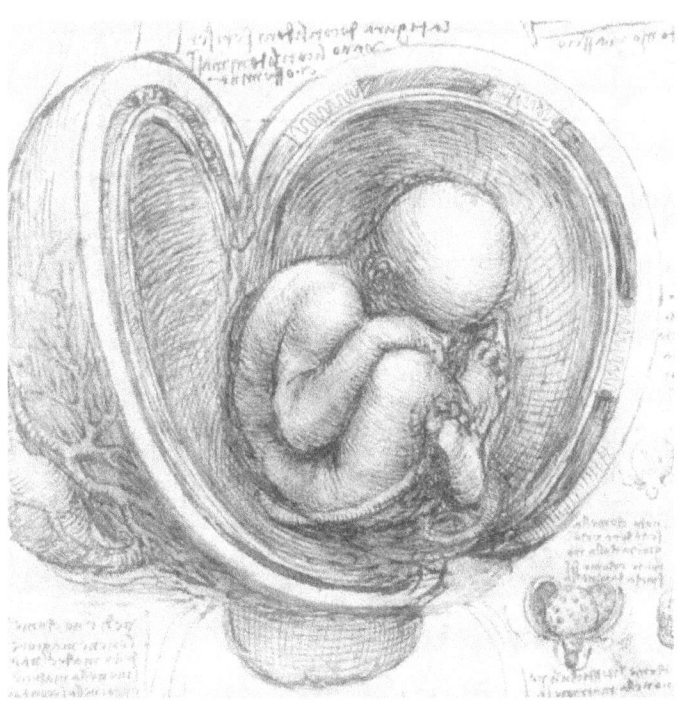

Did you know that Leonardo da Vinci knew more about the human body than most doctors of his day?

How many different sketches of the human body do you see here? ☐
(These are just a small sample of the ones he drew!)
　　　　Do you regonize the different parts of the body in each sketch? ☐

Which is your favorite? Sketch it here:

Leonardo disected at least thirty human bodies over the years?
(Why do you think he disected so many?)

☐

Do you think he approached art as a scientist or science as an artist?
(Or maybe both?) ☐

Leonardo wrote the following about the human foot:
　　"The human foot is a masterpiece of engineering and a work of art."
Do you agree or disagree? ☐

Go back to the **Paintings** page. At least one of these paintings really shows Leonardo's study of anatomy. Find one and explain why you chose it:

☐

22

Leonardo's Last Supper

Q and A

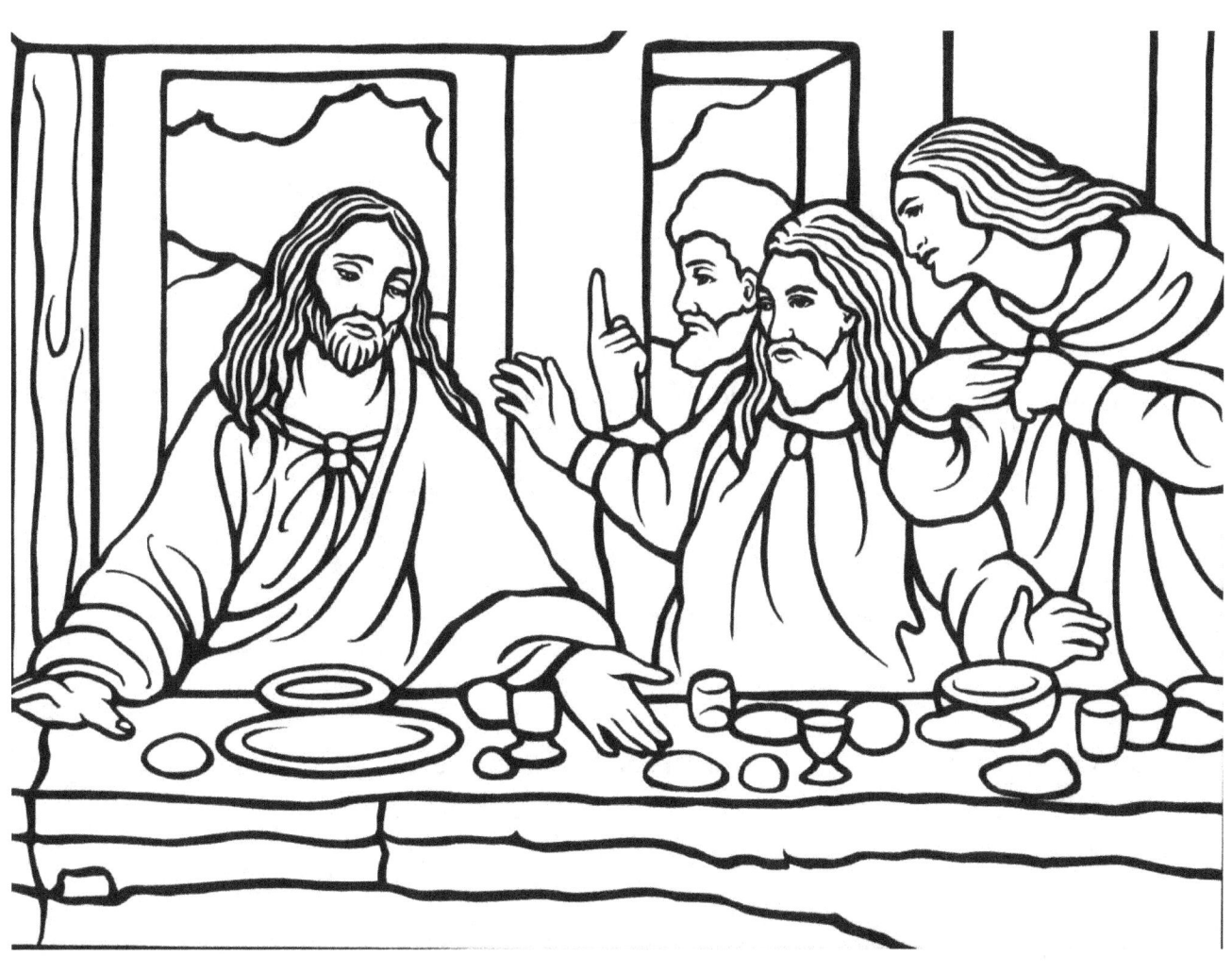

Did you know – the Last Supper is a mural, but it is not a fresco?
Did you know the Last Supper is almost 30 feet wide?
See if you can figure out later how wide that is!

Look closely at Leonardo's **Last Supper** – it was neither the first or the most recent, but it is definitely the most famous!

1. How are the disciples grouped?

2. Can you see the blue at both ends of the tablecloth? They were much more obvious when Leonardo painted the Last Supper.

3. What can you see on the table in front of the disciples?

4. What colors are in the robe Christ is wearing?

5. Did Leonardo paint Christ with a halo? Why or why not?

6. About how long did it take Leonardo to paint the Last Supper?

7. Can you tell what happened to the bottom of the painting sometime after that?

8. Did you know that a twenty-two year restoration of the Last Supper was finished in 1999? Much work was done on the Last Supper to remove 500 years of grime, as well as paint that other painters had added over the years to try to "fix" it.

Leonardo da Vinci and Animals

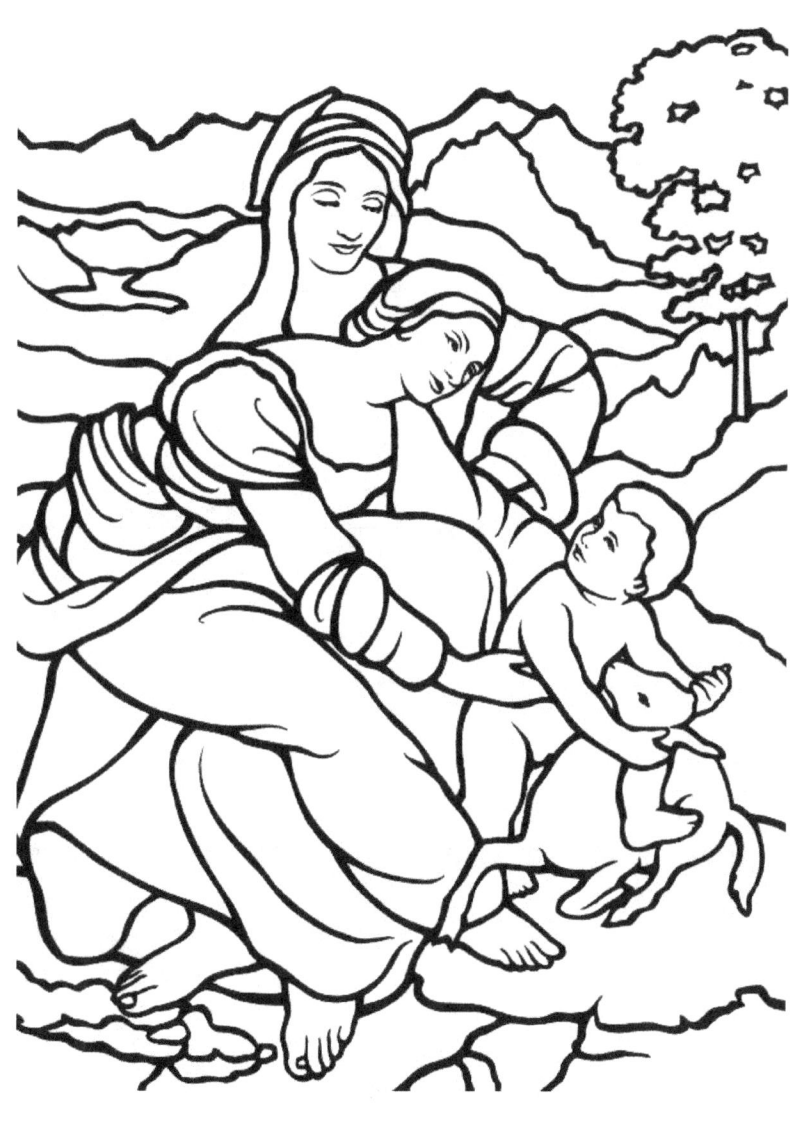

Leonardo liked animals so much that he became a vegetarian (at a time that very few people were). He also liked to draw animals. Many of Leonardo's sketches and paintings include animals.

Locate several of them, draw or write the names below, and where you found them:

Here are a few other animal drawings by Leonardo da Vinci. Circle your favorite:

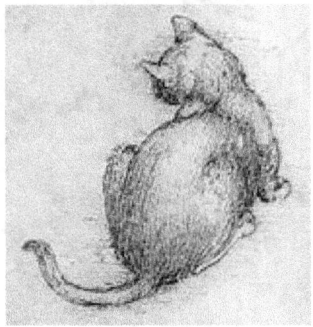 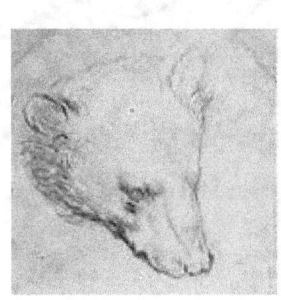 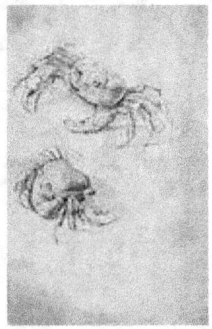

Leonardo and His Horse Sculpture Scavenger Hunt

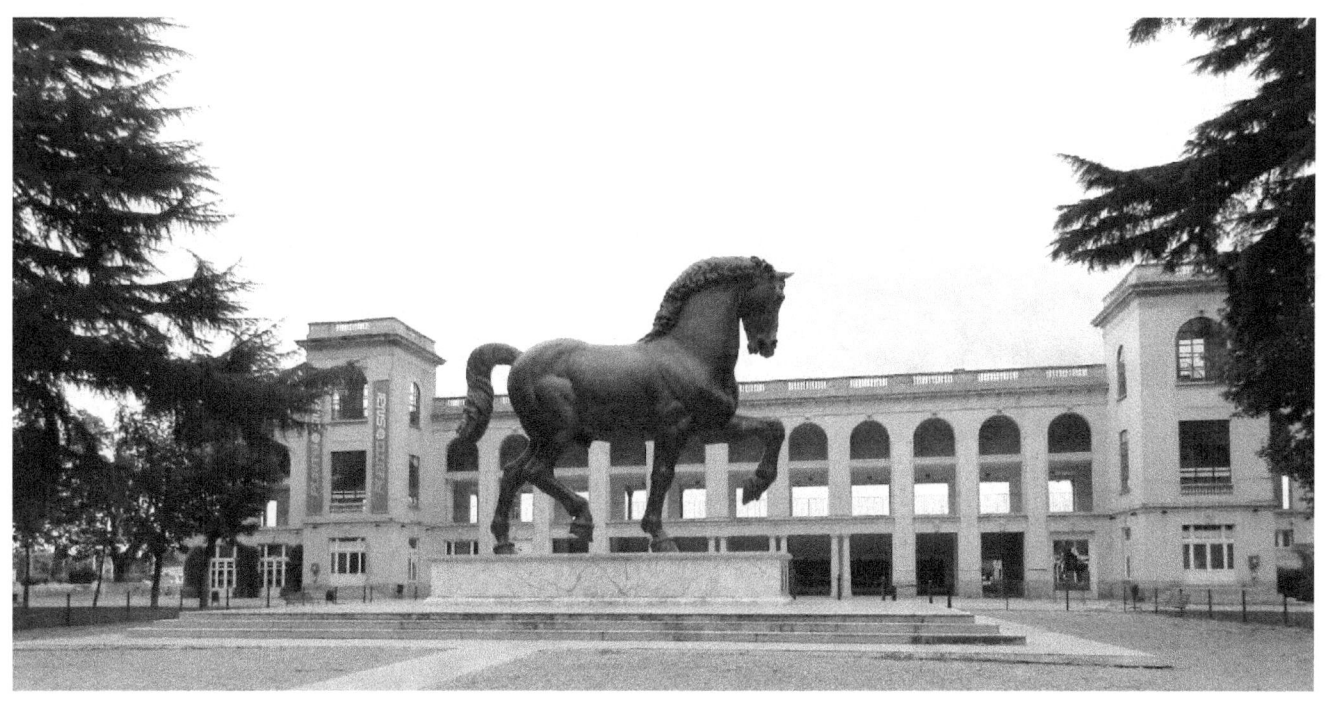

The Horse Sculpture in Milan, Italy

Leonardo learned about sculpting while he was an apprentice under Verrocchio in Florence. When he moved to Milan, he wrote a letter to the Duke, offering to make an equestrian (horse) sculpture for the Duke (in memory of his father).

When did Leonardo start work on sketches for the sculpture?

How big was the equestrian sculpture supposed to be?

What did Leonardo finally finish in 1493?

Whose attack of Milan brought an end to Leonardo's work on his monument?

Leonardo's horse was finally cast in 1999 in Grand Rapids, Michigan. You can see a copy there or in Milan, Italy.

Sketch one of Leonardo's horses below:

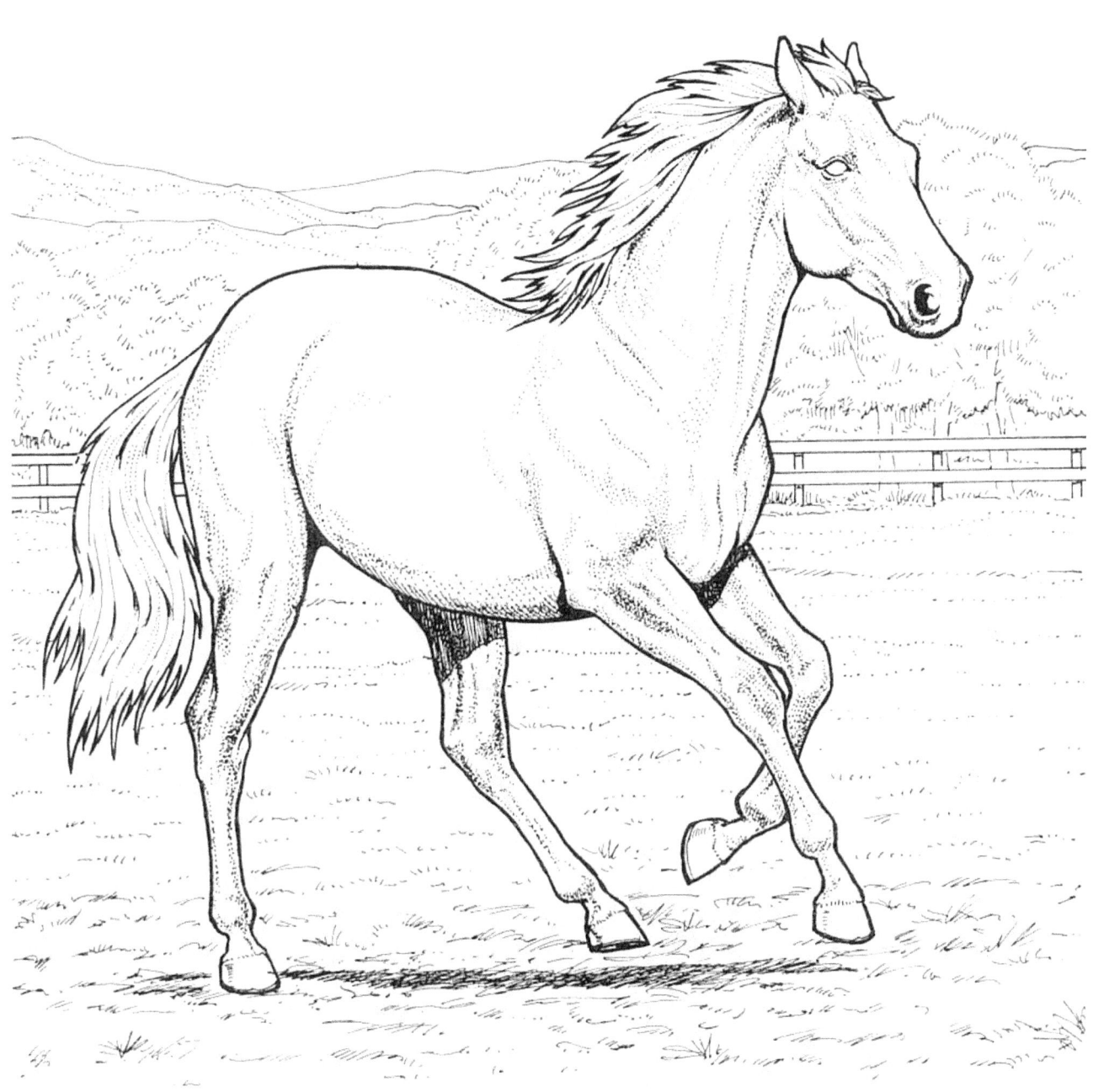

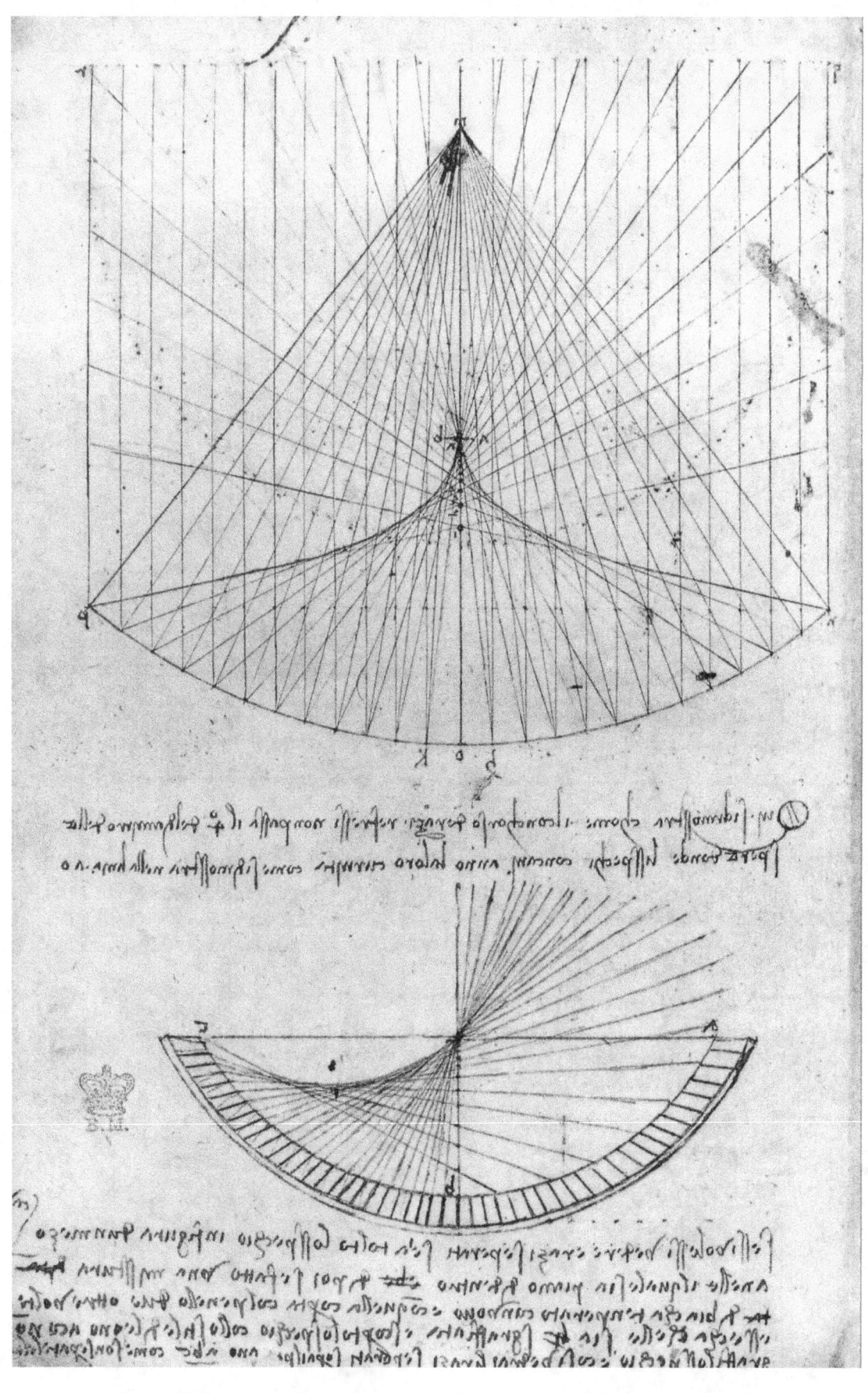

One of the many, many pages from Leonardo's Notebooks

Hydraulic and Aquatic Studies

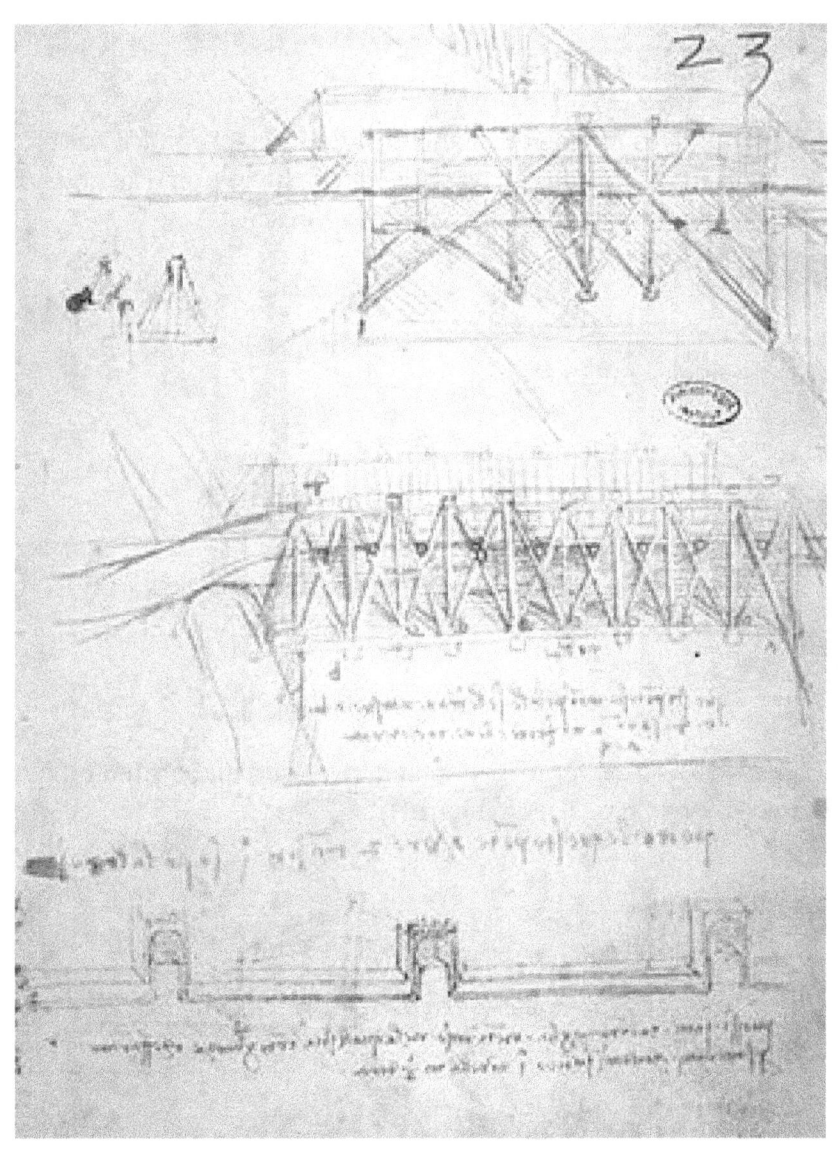

"Water is the driving force of all nature."

Water was especially important during the Middle Ages and the Renaissance. Leonardo studied water on and off for decades. He helped build canals in Milan and tried to divert the River Arno while he was in Florence.

Look at the pictures of his bridge designs. Which is your favorite? Sketch it here:

In addition to designs for bridges for the duke and Cesare Borgia, Leonardo also designed a bridge for the Ottoman Sultan, Bajazeth II. This design was thought to be impractical and was not attempted for almost 500 years – until Vebjorn Sand built it recently in Norway.

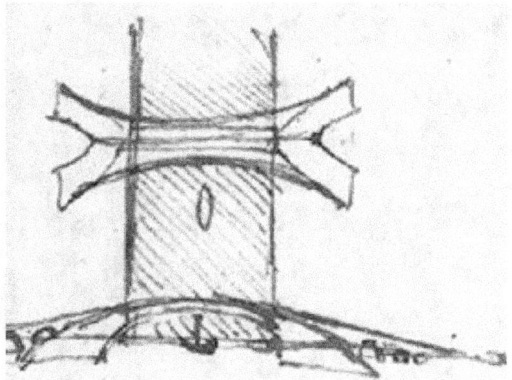

Leonardo's Design for the Sultan

Archimedes invented a water screw for irrigation and Leonardo elaborated on it. Find Leonardo's sketch of the Archimedes Screw and sketch it here:

Leonardo once wrote, "There are three classes of people: Those who see. Those who see when they are shown. Those who do not see." What type of person do you think he considered himself?

A Sample of Leonardo Quotes

"Man is the model of the world."

"He who thinks little errs much."

"Learning never exhausts the mind."

"Iron rusts from disuse, stagnant water loses its purity and in cold weather becomes frozen; even so does inaction sap the vigor of the mind."

"He who despises painting despises philosophy and nature."

"Simplicity is the ultimate sophistication."

"Art is never finished, only abandoned."

"There are three classes of people: those who see; those who see when they are shown; those who do not see."

"The noblest pleasure is the joy of understanding."

"The human foot is a masterpiece of engineering and a work of art."

"I have been impressed with the urgency of doing. Knowing is not enough; we must apply. Being willing is not enough; we must do."

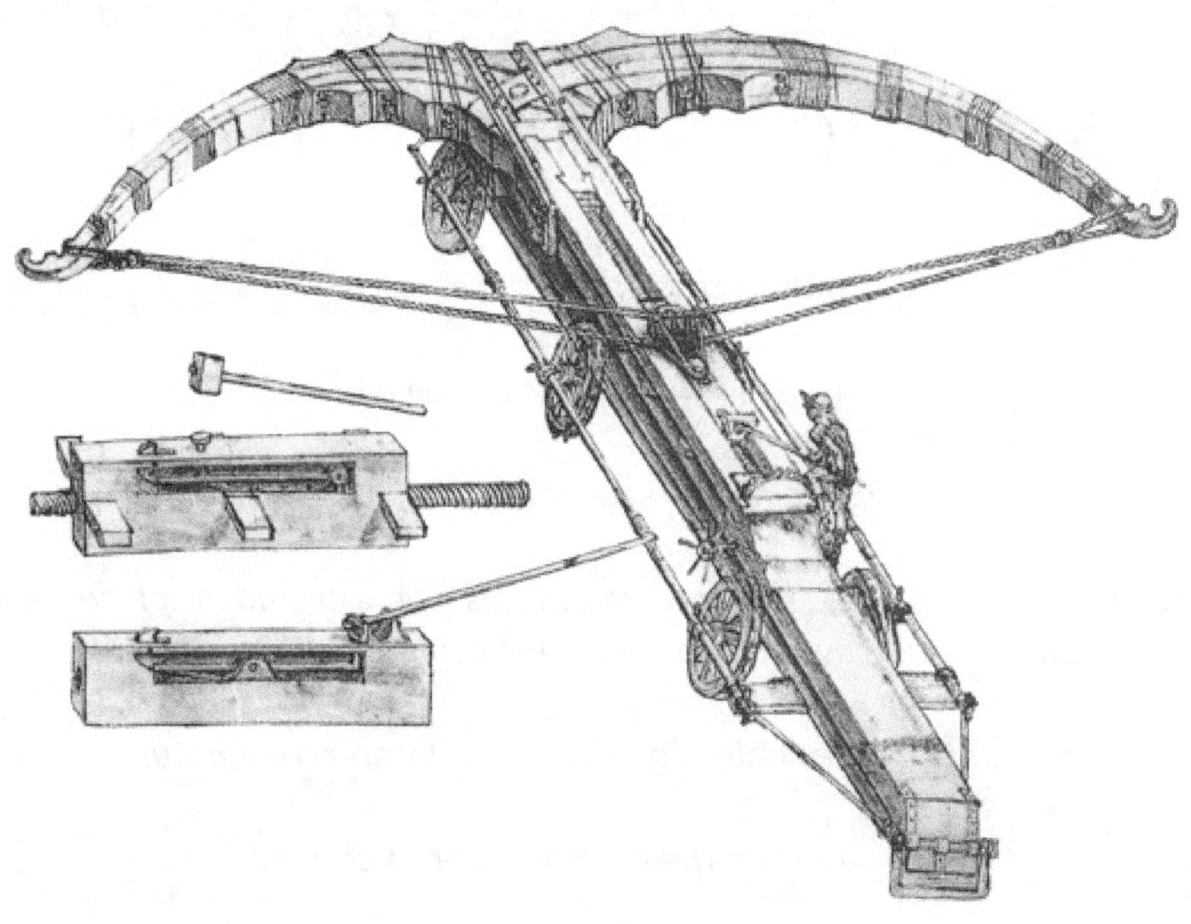

Leonardo, the Military Advisor

My Notes and Sketches

www.ingramcontent.com/pod-product-compliance
Lightning Source LLC
Chambersburg PA
CBHW081808170526
45167CB00008B/3379